Wizard Poems

Fiona Waters is a highly accomplished anthologist and is Editorial Director of Troubadour. She has worked with children's books for over thirty-five years.

Margaret Chamberlain has been a full-time illustrator since leaving the Royal College of Art. She lives by the sea in Lyme Regis with her husband, who is also an illustrator.

Wizard Poems

CHOSEN BY
FIONA WATERS

Illustrated by Margaret Chamberlain

MACMILLAN CHILDREN'S BOOKS

For Neil Hambleton with affection and gratitude.

First published 2004 by Macmillan Children's Books
a division of Macmillan Publishers Limited
20 New Wharf Road, London N1 9RR
Basingstoke and Oxford
www.panmacmillan.com

Associated companies throughout the world

ISBN 0 330 43330 X

1 3 5 7 9 8 6 4 2

A CIP catalogue record for this book is available from
the British Library.

Printed and bound in Great Britain by Mackays of Chatham plc, Kent

Contents

The Two Wizards

The Wizard of the Northland,
   He came to visit me.
He blew in as a snow-storm;
   So I became a tree
     (A leafless tree).

Then he became a Polar ship
   And I became the keel;
So he became a walrus,
   And I a barking seal
     (A young grey seal).

Then he became an icicle,
   So I became a flame.
Then he became a howling wind,
   And I became the same
     (The very same).

And together we blew,
   Together we blew,
   Till nobody knew
Which was I and which was he.
   And neither did we.
     Neither did we.

Gerard Benson

The Wizard's Book

If you want to read his Spell Book
You must take it by surprise . . .

It watches from the bookshelf
With its fierce and inky eyes
It hears your softest footfall
With its folded, paper ears,
It sniffs your fear like perfume,
And it feeds on children's tears.

It lurks in dust and shadows
Where it waits for musty ages
To trap your prying fingers
In its swift and vicious pages,
It tempts you with its secrets
It lures the quick and clever

It lets you think you've won the game
Then snap – you're lost forever!

Clare Bevan

Lost

I've been up on the roof and out to the shed,
Looked in the bathroom
And under the bed.

I've checked by the TV and all the book cases,
The back of the sofa
And other strange places.

I've hunted through the wardrobe and all the drawers,
I've ripped up the carpets
And examined the floors.

I've looked in the freezer and washing machine,
I've doubled-checked every place
That I've been.

I've turned out the rooms in my wizard's lair
But I can't find
My invisible hat anywhere.

John Coldwell

The Magician's Robe

Deepest blue velvet
The colour of midnight
Fur-lined to keep out the cold,
Spangled with silver moons,
Stars, constellations,
Symbols and signs worked in gold –
Mine is a fine robe
With long narrow pockets.
Who knows what secrets they hold?

Sue Cowling

Just Practising

We came to where his strange house stood:
A clearing deep within the wood.
Behind an ivy-covered tree
We crouched with thumping hearts to see:
First, where the house had been, a space,
Then following quickly in its place:
A thundercloud, a storm, a blizzard,
An elephant, a giant lizard,
An ape, a bear, an octopus,
A truck, a double-decker bus,
A crocodile, an express train –
And then the wizard's house again.
A waiting stillness, then we saw
Opening wide, the wizard's door.
And out he walked with smiling face,
Looking towards our hiding place.
In a slight bow inclined his head:
'Just practising,' the wizard said.

Eric Finney

A Point Worth Raising . . .

I wonder
if under
a wizard's

his head is really *shaped* like that!

Graham Denton

Love Letter – From the Wizard to the Witch

I find your looks bewitching,
The way you stand and glare.
I love the way you shake your locks
Of tangled, matted hair.

I find your smile enchanting,
Your wicked, evil grin.
It makes me want to touch and stroke
Your gnarled and wrinkled skin.

I find your face spellbinding,
The warts upon your cheek,
So hairy, black and crusty –
They make my knees go weak.

I find you so enthralling.
I love your witchy smell
Of rats and dung and sewers –
You hold me in your spell!

John Foster

The Not That Willing Worker

I wish I'd stuck to what I knew
and just sat on the mat.
I wish I'd never answered
that advert in *The Daily Cat*.

'Wanted – Willing Worker
for 'Offbeat Type' in pointy hat.
Exciting post – with puffs of smoke –
Magic milk – Designer cloak.
Splendid pay – short exam –
must know words like "Zap-shaz-am".'

What wasn't mentioned were 'the spells',
the cobweb cakes, the test-tube smells.
No reference in the interview
about the meals of spider stew,
but most of all – the awful con –
the fact that I'd be practised on.

These past few weeks I've been a bat,
a frog, but sadly not a cat.
My whiskers now count up to none,
I don't know where my tail has gone.
Tonight, I scurry, without fur,
a cockroach – trying hard to purr.

I wish I'd stuck to what I knew
and just sat on the mat.
I wish I'd never answered
that advert in *The Daily Cat*.

Stewart Henderson

What the Wizened Wizard Was

That wizened whiskered wizard was a really wicked wizard,
That whiskered wizened wizard really was!
He changed a sheep into a leopard
And it went and ate a shepherd,
Oh what a a wicked wizened wizard
That wizened whiskered wicked wizard really was!

Brian Patten

Advice to Young Wizards

Unicorns are born
with *tiny* horns,
even dragons
have to learn
how to breathe flame;

so don't blame
me, if your first spell
doesn't bring you fame,
by turning lead to gold.

Merlin wasn't always
quite so old
or quite so wise;
take my advice,
aim for something
less likely to make
mistakes,
like changing water into ice.

Slip cubes into your
slugslime- and frogspawn-shake;
relax.
    Try another slice
of goblin cake.
Keep cool,
take things easy and you'll
love your years
at wizard school.

Mike Johnson

I Know a Wizard's Garden

I know a Wizard's garden
   where whispering breezes blow,
      where silver fish swim in a pond
      and moonshine flowers grow.

      I know a Wizard's garden
    where blue birds come and go,
  where golden plums hang from the bough
and sometimes there is snow.

I know a Wizard's garden
   where cockerels strut and crow,
      where chocolate cats snooze in the shade
      and singing streamlets flow.

Wes Magee

Song of the Wizard's Imp

Catch me if you can,
I'm a whisper of air,
a splinter of sunlight
that's gone if you stare.

Catch me if you can,
I'm a shadowy patch,
a rustle of cobweb
that's gone if you snatch.

Catch me if you can,
but be sure that you dare,
for I nestle to rest
in a wizard's warm hair.

Yes, catch me if you can,
but be warned I am weird,
for I settle to sleep
in the wizard's white beard.

Oh, catch me if you can,
but don't wake the wizard.
He'll glare and he'll growl
and you'll end up a lizard.

Tony Mitton

Finding the Magic

You don't have to be a wizard
To find the magic.
This life can be sweet, can be hard,
Can be comic or tragic.

You don't need a beard, a wand
Or a pointy hat
To discover what lies beyond
The everyday matter of fact.

My grandfather could cast a spell
When he told me stories or jokes
And I had a teacher who could as well.
They didn't need spangled cloaks.

What they did was help me to see
How magic lies all around
And that nothing is ordinary,
That we share an uncommon ground.

So, wizards, I tell you this,
For all your special powers,
What's truly magical is
The world that's already ours,

The world in which every day
Is so different, so various,
That whatever your spell books say
It's *you* who have need of *us*!

John Mole

A Wizard Blizzard

(or Watch Out for the Peaked Hats)

Wizards flew to a wizard convention;
Through the sky with their wands they went gliding.
It took 20 air-traffic controllers
Just to keep the whole bunch from colliding.

Robert Scotellaro

On a Guided Tour of Camelot

That bloke over there? Why, that's Merlin.

Note the star-spangled cloak he's unfurling
And the way his white whiskers are curling
And the wand which he's constantly twirling
With rubies and mother-of-pearl in.

See the mist round his feet, how that's curling?
Well, when he casts a spell, it starts swirling;
But then, when it's curses he's hurling,
You should see the speed it's set whirling!

Nick Toczek

The Wizard's Dog

The wizard's dog
doesn't bury bones.
He hides stars.

He doesn't go walkies.
He flies.

He doesn't fetch sticks.
He brings back wands.

But he does chase
the witch's cat.

And when his master gets home
he goes crazy
with excitement and love.

So, in many ways,
he is a fairly ordinary
sort of dog.

The wizard's dog.

Bernard Young

Spellsong

(with respect for John Donne 1572–1631)

Go and save a dying star,
Seek magic from an ash tree root,
Ask me where the Fair Folk are,
Grasp a firebird's feathered foot.
Treasure up a seal's soft singing,
Hold fast to a nettle's stinging,
And find
What wind
Blows spellsongs at a wizard's mind.

Lucy Coats

The Dream Maker

In the woods
   beyond the meadow
where the shadow's
   deep
lives a wizard
   mending, making
traceries
   of sleep.

Soft and gentle
   hard and hoary
where the yaffles
   drum
you may find him
   turning, twisting
finger over
   thumb.

Dreams, he fashions:
   webs of wonder
misty, milky
   white.
Moist and tender
   are his fancies,
delicate
   and light.

In the woods
    beyond the meadow
you must walk
    alone
if you want
    to come upon him
crouching
    by a stone.

Weaving out of
    threads of nothing
something strange
    and rare.
Mice and spiders
    feed his silence,
and the green
    air.

Jean Kenward

Do You Want to Be a Wizard?

Do you want to be a wizard?
    Well, you'll need a pointed hat
    with silver stars and golden moon,
    and perched on top . . . a bat.

Do you want to be a wizard?
    Well, you'll need *Ye Booke of Spells*
    and rotten eggs and fried frog's legs
    to make some horrid smells.

Do you want to be a wizard?
    Well, you'll need some pickled brains,
    a wand, a cloak, and one dead rat,
    and green slime from the drains.

Do you *still* want to be a wizard?

Wes Magee

29

Wizard McBoffin's Amazing Creations

Self-cleaning socks for long-distance runners
Self-cooling sandals for steaming hot summers
Bedsocks for dogs, fatter pillows for cats
Spring-loaded exocet-strength cricket bats
Self-inflating life-saving knickers
Pulpits with engines for overworked vicars
All these and more – the newest sensations
Wizard McBoffin's amazing creations!

Bananas and oranges fitted with zips
Healthy calorie-free fish and chips
Centrally heated warm toilet seats
Non-flavour-fading non-shrinking sweet sweets
A homework computer that fits in the pocket
Football boots with power of a rocket
All these and more – the newest sensations
Wizard McBoffin's amazing creations!

With sprockets and sockets and test tubes that boil
Wires and fires, foil and oil,
Springs that go zing and things that uncoil
Wizard McBoffin's all trial and toil

Jottings and workings and odd calculations
Diagrams labelled with weird notations
Models that move with the strangest rotations
Wizard McBoffin knows no limitations

Wizard McBoffin – a man with a mission
Wizard McBoffin – a plan and a vision
Wizard McBoffin – a star you can wish on

There's no one quite like him – Wizard McBoffin
Inventive inventions with lots of good stuff in
So much information that we can learn off him

A brain and a mind beyond contemplation
Wizard McBoffin's amazing creations!

Paul Cookson

A Wizard's Spell To Make Your School Day Shorter

(From *The Great Book of Spells*, Chapter Seven:
'How to Get Out of Going to School')

Take a pinch of chalk dust
A spoonful of yellow paint
Five hairs from the caretaker's beard
Two hairs from the dinner lady's moustache
A handful of pencil shavings
A big squirt of glue, a small bottle of ink
Three nouns and some cloudy tap water
Ten drops of sweat from a greasy trainer
A smattering of verbs
Some broken up fractions
A used times-table, (eights are best)
A dollop of lumpy custard from dinner time
Mix in a teacher's shout
An early morning yawn
The chatter of children
A head teacher's glare
The spring of a stopwatch
Six wet playtimes
And thirteen rings of the school bell.

Stir it all up with a wooden ruler
And whisper;

This is a Wizard's Spell
Make sure you learn it well
Move the clock on the wall
Let there be no time at all
For sums or Literacy
Wizard, set us free
As I stir this special brew
Wizard, do what you must do!

Wait five minutes and count to a thousand
As the mixture bubbles
Watch all the clock hands whiz and spin
Then the home-time bell rings out
And you are free.
Yippeeeeee!

Wizard Warning;
Always do this spell at morning playtime
And only do it once or twice a week
Otherwise somebody will catch on.

David Harmer

The Wizard's Cat

When the wizard cast
a spell on his cat,
he was tired, it backfired
and now this cat
is only half the creature
it used to be,
but half a cat
is still company
still purrs, still warms
the wizard's seat,
still rubs round his legs
and gets under his feet.
But half a cat
Is disconcerting
for other cats
when fighting or flirting.
It's doubly feared
this weird half-cat,
this half invisible
acrobat.

The wizard is worried
he knows that he should
redo the spell
and make it good.
But what would be left
if this spell should fail?
How much of his cat,
maybe only a tail.
The wizard too
might be incomplete,
just a wizard's legs
and a wizard's feet.
So best not to meddle
with what's been done,
surely half a cat
is better than none.

Brian Moses

Should a Wizard Swish By in a Cloak of Invisibility

A flicker in the fire
A shimmer in the air
A flutter in a cobweb
A sudden feline stare

A shadow cast in starlight
A pricking canine ear
A tremor in your teacup
All tell that he passed near.

Philip Waddell

The Search for Silence

The Wizard turned a final, rustling page
And found that he needed
One Minute Of Silence
To complete his spectacular spell.
So, he oiled the creaky door;
Hung a cloth of darkness over the cuckoo clock;
Fed the owl a handful of sweet dreams,
And froze the flames of his astonished fire.
Then he waited for nothingness to begin.

But the toad wheezed;
The spiders munched their sleepy supper,
The apple tree tickled the window with its rattly fingers.
So, the Wizard tucked a silver box inside his starry sleeve
And set off to search for Silence.

He entered the centre of the deepest forest,
Where the winds moaned
And the wild beasts snuffled round his slippers.
He dived below the drowsy waters,
Where lonely whales warbled their mournful song
And blue lobsters snapped with grumpy claws.
He stumbled across the snowy wastes where white bears snored.
He explored lost cities and the tombs of long-dead kings,
But everywhere he heard the thud, thud of his hopeful heart
And the swish of his own, disappointed robes.

At last, he shuffled home.
He stroked the toad,
Placed his empty box on a high shelf
And fell sadly asleep.
Now he stepped inside a silent world
Where no nightingales trilled,
No bands crashed and boomed,
No sleigh bells jingled.
Toast didn't crunch,
Bats couldn't squeak,
Parrots wouldn't squawk,
There were no carol singers,
No purring cats,
No sizzling sausages,

No fizzing fireworks,
Everyone walked on the very tips of their toes,
And no one ever laughed, or whistled,
Or whispered a kindly word.

When the alarm-hen clucked,
The Wizard sat up and cried,
'Who needs this silly spell anyway?'
He ripped the last page from his book
And let it crackle on the delighted fire.
Then he filled his silver box with music
And skipped away to hunt for happiness instead.

Clare Bevan

You Can't Be That

I told them:
When I grow up
I'm not going to be a scientist
Or someone who reads the news on TV.
No, a million birds will fly through me.
I'M GOING TO BE A TREE.

They said,
You can't be that. No, you can't be that.

I told them:
When I grow up
I'm not going to be an airline pilot,
A dancer, a lawyer or an MC.
No, huge whales will swim in me.
I'M GOING TO BE AN OCEAN!

They said,
You can't be that. No, you can't be that.

I told them:
I'm not going to be a DJ,
A computer programmer, a musician or a beautician.
No, streams will flow through me, I'll be the home of eagles;
I'll be full of nooks, crannies, valleys and fountains.
I'M GOING TO BE A RANGE OF MOUNTAINS!

They said,
You can't be that. No, you can't be that.

I asked them:
Just what do you think I am?
Just a child, they said,
And children always become
At least one of the things
We want them to be.

They do not understand me.
I'll be a stable if I want, smelling of fresh hay,
I'll be a lost glade where unicorns still play.
They do not realize that I can fulfil any ambition.
They do not realize among them
Walks a magician.

Brian Patten

Problem Potion

Merlin made a magic potion.
Started off with bee-sting lotion.
Added bugs' blood, skins of lizards,
bullocks' eyeballs, chickens' gizzards,
deadly nightshade, stewed molasses.
Pumped it full of sulphur gases.
Wicked smell! Could not ignore it.
Trouble was, how could he store it?

Sticky, flammable, corrosive.
Dangerous as high explosive.
Volatile, asphyxiating.
Burnt its way through armour-plating.
Barrels blazed and turned to ashes.
Bottles fizzed with dazzling flashes.
Metal drums it split asunder,
bursting with a roar like thunder.

Yet, in spite of all the flurry,
Merlin had no need to worry.
While he stood and meditated
all the stuff evaporated.

Barry Buckingham

44

Wizard Acrostic

Wonderfully wise
In knowledge of the
Zodiac,
An ancient astrologer and adviser,
Reciter of chants
Delivering enchantment.

Debjani Chatterjee

Don't You Think . . .

A wizard's wand seems rather thin

for holding on too tightly?

Graham Denton

The Apothecary

Lotions, potions, herbs and spices,
These are what he sells.
Just ignore the heated floor,
The pungent, drifting smells.

Don't go down the cellar steps
To see what lies below.
Turn your eyes from flasks and jars –
It's better not to know.

Don't inspect his crystal ball,
His telescope or globe.
Don't stir his experiments
Or try his wizard's robe.

Don't disturb his book of spells
Or touch his quill and chart.
Don't believe he practises
A dark forbidden art.

Sue Cowling

The Missing Wish

Wiz wished he had a wand-less wish,
his wanton wand to find
for it had wandered out of hand,
which troubled Wiz's mind.

'Twas 'ard for Wiz to live without
his wand that disappeared –
like only half of him was there,
and most of that was beard.

Wiz was distraught, wished he were dead
but with no wand to wave
he couldn't grant himself this wish.
His problem, it was grave

and wand-less-ly, Wiz wandered on
from wand to wand . . . poor bloke,
the wand that had got out of hand
was only in his cloak!

Gina Douthwaite

Wizard on the Line

My father is a wizard
he gets the eight-o-two
hat and wand
   and black cape
   from Fleet to Waterloo.
He keeps his spells in a Thermos
but dropped the lot last week,
squeezing past some people
fighting for a seat.

Commuters turned to turnips
others turned to slugs
some turned right into tigers
and others into bugs.

The scene was really awful
the guard began to whine
–'This train will stop at Clapham –
there's a wizard on the line.'

Peter Dixon

The Rain Man

I am the rain man

I walk these hills

Look in my hands
these clouds
are grey flowers
brimming tearful with pain

I bring you
this whisper
at the shuddering crossroads
where the eye of the ley-line
touches spiralling lanes

and I bring you
dark birds
broken branches
cracked lightning

I bring you
this silence
this echo
this handclap

I bring you

the rain

David Greygoose

Wizard Wood

Is that a wizard's breath
stirring small fresh leaves
in the touching treetops
into new growth,
moving grasses?

No, only the spring breeze
shaking itself after winter,
warming up.

Is that a wizard's footprint
caught in the leaf-mould mud,
flattening the last of the bluebells,
disappearing under bramble heaps,
along rabbit tracks?

No, only the steps of children
lost in a rich green world,
playing hide-and-seek.

Is that a wizard's hand
plucking ripe berries,
brushing red and gold leaves,
sending larch and pine cones
tumbling brackenward?

No, only squirrels harvesting autumn,
hustling, bustling,
before tucking themselves up.

Is that a wizard's tall shadow
– bent hat, twisted arms –
leaning out from behind
the old yew tree
shattered with age.

No, only the winter sun
casting shades of sleep
over the resting earth.

This *must* be a wizard's magic,
the whole wood turned white;
no birdsong, no rustling, just
    ice cracking
    snow plopping
    stream trickling
    quietly by
    frost-frozen twigs
    stars twinkling
    a bright silver moon.

And look, over there,
a shape almost melting
into the snow between trees;
   white beard
   white cloak
   diamond-bright eyes
   arms spread wide . . .

That's him!

Perhaps.

Patricia Leighton

The Magician

The magician at Daphne's party
Was called The Great Zobezank
But we knew it was only Daphne's dad
Who worked at the Westminster Bank.

He waved his wand and told us all,
'I need a volunteer.
Who'll step inside my magic box
And mysteriously disappear?'

We shouted, 'Mister, hey, Mister, please choose me'
And waved our arms like mad
But he chose Daphne Smartyboots
Because he was her dad.

He raised his little magic wand
And waved it in the air
And when he opened his magic box
Daphne wasn't there

He bowed and smiled, while Daphne's mum
Shouted 'Bravo' and cheered
Then Zobezank shouted the magic words
To make Daphne re-appear.

But when he opened that magic door
No Daphne stood inside
And her father muttered, 'Oh deary me'
While her mother wailed and cried.

They called, 'Oh, Daphne dear, where are you?'
And beat upon the door
But as for us we clapped and cheered
Louder than before.

Gareth Owen

Midnight Rune

By midnight's moon
a river ran rune
and a blue-white swan was gliding.
And the silver leaves of a golden tree
shook as the stars went riding.

John Rice

The Wizard

On the black rocks by the bay,
A tower rises gaunt and grey.
It is the home, so people say,
Of the Wizard of the West.

The castle walls are sheer and high,
Its turrets touch the very sky,
And every window's like an eye
Of some great towering beast.

And in that fort of gaunt grey stone
The wizard sits there all alone,
And glowers from his granite throne
And dreams of dreadful deeds.

A tangled mane grows from his head,
Above grey eyes as dull as lead,
Around the mouth – a slit of red –
And a hard and hook-like nose.

His beard is long and snowy white,
His cloak is blacker than the night,
Spangled with stars, which catch the light,
And golden mystic shapes.

With silver wand he weaves his spell,
And chants the charms he knows so well,
A magic he will never tell,
To any living soul.

Hocus-pocus, magic potions,
Mumbo-jumbo, good-luck lotions,
With his wand he waves and motions,
Around his bubbling pot.

He turns a fly into a frog,
Transforms a spider to a dog,
Summons up a swirling fog,
Or whistles up the wind.

With magic belt and lucky stone,
Moonstone ring and wishing bone,
The wizard conjures all alone
In his gaunt grey tower.

When all the fields are swathed in snow,
And round the wall the cold winds blow,
And the moonlight casts an eerie glow,
You'll hear him in his tower.

On the black rocks by the bay,
A tower rises gaunt and grey,
It is the home, so people say,
Of the Wizard of the West.

Gervase Phinn

Whizz Kid

Did you hear
About the wizard
Who came from Outer Space?
He was just
A *flying sorcerer*
With stardust on his face.

Clive Webster

The Brown Bear

In the dark wood
In a clearing
Sleeps a brown bear
Dreaming, dreaming

His skin is furless
His paws are clawless
He walks into the city
Lawless, lawless

The moon is hidden
The clouds are weeping
A princess slumbers
Sleeping, sleeping

The thief creeps through
The royal bedroom
And steals her ruby
A priceless heirloom

The ruby glows
With fire and lightning
A spell is cast
So frightening, frightening

The thief grows fur
His body thickens
His hands grow claws
He sickens, sickens

Beneath the black sky
Thunder rumbles
Into the dark wood
He stumbles, stumbles

For in the ruby,
Gleaming, gleaming
A wizard's mind
Is scheming, scheming

Now, in the dark wood
In a clearing
Sleeps a brown bear
Dreaming, dreaming

Roger Stevens

The Spell of Kuruxan

When you walked down the passage what did you see?
    A door with a message that I knew was for me.

What did you find when you opened the door?
    An old wooden chest in the middle of the floor.

What did you find when you opened the lid?
    A parcel of paper sealed with wax that was red.

What did you find when you opened the seal?
    A portrait of Kuruxan, looking powerful – and real.

What did you see when you looked in his eyes?
    A stare that went through me and saw all my lies.

And what will you do now when you hear the dark bells?
    I will come when he calls me – and do as he tells . . .

Trevor Millum

Flight

Lord Saffron put aside his willow wand,
Stretched and took off his long conical hat,
Shook loose the planets and stars
And scooped them into a drawer.

He hung his magic robe woven with moons
On the hook on the study door;
Then shut and sealed his book of spells.
(No need to mark his place. The book would know.)

He opened the green glass window wide
And Abanastra, his companion crow,
Cawed and shook out her blue-black wings
And flew to the oak, to rest.

The wizard went outside to tend his herbs,
And thinking, stared – at herbs, at pond,
Then at the wall, last at the open sky.
Perhaps one day, he thought, perhaps one day . . .

One far-off day it might be possible
To build a machine that would fly.
He laughed. But not today.
Today he'd just have to make do.

Make do with the old, old ways.
Lifting his arms he fell into a trance.
Soon he was soaring high above the hill
While Abanastra watched from the ancient tree.

Gerard Benson

The Prisoner

The Wizard lies frozen,
unchanged by time,
lost in a place
where spells cease to rhyme,
where memories fade
and where thoughts spark, then die.
Rare crystals surround him
and golden chains tie
him down to a black rock.
A swift silver stream
spins enchantments around him.
He wanders in dreams
but sometimes, as years
go whispering by,
the Wizard breathes, 'Arthur'
soft as a sigh.

Marian Swinger

The Winter Wizard

Unheard, unseen,
The Winter Wizard roams the country
And the town,
His long white cloak of eiderdown
Streaming out behind.
His wand's a frond of ice
And nothing's spared its chilling touch:
Plants change from green
To black and brown, and pools and ponds
Solidify. Everywhere you go
Where Winter Wizard goes you'll find
Something has changed
Quite magically. Even the ground
Glistens like a million tiny diamonds
Or a star-strewn galaxy
After Winter Wizard's been around.

But make the most of Winter Wizard's magic
While you can, for you know
He'll go eventually.
He only stays for several months
Before another wizard comes along,
Dressed head to toe
In beaten gold, his wand
A budding twig.
He'll undo all Winter Wizard's spells
And cast spells of his own
And, once again, everything will change
Quite magically . . .

Gillian Floyd

The Castle of
Spells and Wishes

High high above the earth,
deep deep below the sky,
wizards, magicians, sorcerers
circle and hover above
the Castle of Spells and Wishes
in air that smells of strawberries.

A pillar of sunlight for a stairway,
a beam of moonlight for a flagpole,
a circle of sparkling liquid jewels for a moat.

Castle walls, thick as cliffs,
protect the King and Queen
in their controllable kingdom.
For them a fortified town to play in,
a silent church to pray in,
and a dark dungeon to conceal their fears.

A flame of oakfire for messages,
a flock of doves for newsbringers,
a jester without a tongue for happiness.

High high above the earth,
deep deep below the sky,
wizards, magicians, sorcerers
circle and hover above
the Castle of Spells and Wishes
in air that smells of sulphur.

John Rice

The Wizard Who Isn't

Nobody wants magic these days
Sighed the sad old wizard
Sitting alone
In his home in the wood.
It's no good, he went on.
Magic's old hat.
At nine hundred and ninety-nine years of age
I'm redundant, unemployed, on the dole
And that's that.

So the wizard who isn't
(At least, not any more)
Burnt all his books
(Of which there were many)
And broke all his wands
Till he didn't have any.
He finally took off his hat and his cloak
And set them on fire. *There*, he said
As they went up in smoke.
From now on I'll just be an ordinary bloke;

So that's what he became.
The wizard who isn't
Left his home in the wood
And went to the city,
Where, I'm glad to say, he's doing quite well,
Teaching schoolchildren how to read, write
And spell.

Gillian Floyd

The Wizard's Hat

What is under the wizard's hat:
a cone of ice
sleeping mice
his favourite spell?
Who can tell?

What is under the wizard's hat:
a pile of bones
a tower of stones
a fiendish device?
a passing bell
a red red rose?
Who knows?

What is that under the wizard's hat:
a crust of bread
a book he's read
a bag of groans?
mashed potatoes
loaded dice
a rotten smell?
Can you guess
more or less?

So what is under that wizard's hat:
a ziggurat
a dancing bat?
his pointy head
     an awful mess?
          an unblown overgrown saxophone
          a dozen crows
          a word of advice?
          a caramel, a cockleshell, a
               fond farewell
          a heap of dust?

               No. It's just
               his fat old cat.

Dave Calder

The Very Pointy Wizard

The wizard is a pointy man
with a pointy stick
he wears a pointy hat
and he's got a little trick
of making magic movements
with his podgy pointy hand
turning rabbits into radishes
and sandwiches to sand.

He's got a pointy head
and a purple pointy nose
bushy pointy eyebrows
and fifteen pointy toes
he wiggles and he waggles
his tiny pointy eyes
then disappears with a BOOM!
and takes us by surprise.

He lives a pointy life
in his pointy pointy house
turning ice cream into cabbages
and then he'll turn a mouse
into a fridge and back again
with a potent pointy spell
then it changes to a kipper
with a niffy fishy smell.

If you see him in the street
then it's time to run
he'll point his pointy finger
and magic you for fun
you'll become a parrot
a beetle or a cat
and when you meet your mum
what will she think of that?

David Harmer

Well!

Ding dong bell,
The wizard cast a spell,
But all he got was three deep holes,
Well, well, well.

Ian Larmont

The Wizard's Revenge

(A haiku)

He used to enjoy
Practical jokes – my little
Toad of a brother.

Philip Waddell